SMALL FO

Simple Recipes for Ramekin Cooking
by Bill Fishbourne

Food you'll love,
one serving at a time,
proportioned
just right!

Why?
SMALL FOODS

We started this book for a number of reasons. We're "Baby Boomers" and many of our friends are too. We'd have our friends over for dinner and they would comment that it was hard to cook for just two people. They'd had families who'd grown up and left and now that lasagna they used to make would be weeks worth of leftovers. Additionally their metabolisms were slowing down and they just didn't have the appetite for huge amounts of food any more. They were gaining weight and they didn't know what to do.

The younger set also has a problem. They are marrying later, starting their families later and both spouses are working later to make ends meet. The old days when a worker left at 4:30 or 5:00 are long past. If you do that today you're a prime target for a layoff or missed promotions. Again these young professionals need something small and also quick.

And we're all gaining weight. We eat too much and we tend to eat the wrong things. We need to eat less and ideally get some exercise. You probably won't eat like this seven days a week but 2 or 3 times a week could make a difference.

This book is all about portion control. You're bound to break the rules occasionally and eat some carbs and in fact we use some carbs in our recipes, just to add a taste or texture element. The trick is to make small but very tasty foods. No extra portions, no leftovers, just cook what you need and no more. You can't go back for seconds as there aren't any. If you are used to eating "big", this may seem hard at first. You can fill up on salad (with home made oil and vinegar dressing, not store bought) and hard vegetables like celery or radishes. Keep avoiding high sugar vegetables and fruits like carrots, bananas, etc. Don't add meats, croutons or cheese. Use a salad plate to keep from packing it on. I've seen people build huge, meat and cheese filled, salads on dinner plates and then talk about how their diet was not working even though they were eating light. If you do nothing else portion control is a real start and with exercise it may be all you need.

Cooking with
RAMEKINS

To make this easy we build these recipes around a cooking utensil called a *ramekin*. These are normally used for deserts such as crème brulee or custards. We use a seven or eight ounce ramekin as it seems enough to satisfy the appetite. We use the ramekin both as a baking device and as a measure. Going to have a chicken breast tonight? Cut a piece that fits neatly into the cup (don't fill the cup with the meat). Hamburger?, again, fit into the cup. Fish, eat as much as you want, but no butter or sauces. You're basically controlling calories and fat by controlling portion size.

Cooking a ramekin meal is very easy. The recipes are for two servings but you may get three out of a recipe. For the single person these are ideal, cook two and save one for tomorrow or freeze it. Most Ramekins come with plastic tops. The concept here is portion control, no seconds, no leftovers. You don't have to heat up your whole oven just to cook a couple of these. Use a counter top toaster oven that also does convection baking. These can cook faster than an oven, so watch them the first few times. In a full sized oven place the ramekins on a shelf one or two positions from the top of the oven so the filo will brown. We think many of these (particularly the crab) might make excellent appetizers at a dinner party (mini muffin trays and use normal crab for this not the pricey jumbo stuff).

Our recipes make use of some of the evil white foods, particularly frozen filo dough. You can defrost a packet of this, use a few sheets and refreeze it for use again. We don't use much of this and a couple of sheets are not a lot of carbs. We also use PAM, this helps a lot in those recipes where there is no crust. Without PAM you would never get the food out of the cup in one piece. You can also use a thin coating of olive oil if you wish to substitute. To remove the food from the cup, run a butter knife around the inside edge to separate it from the cup, turn it upside down and gently pry it out if it doesn't just shake or drop out. You can also just eat it out of the cup.

We've cooked all of these recipes time and time again, fine tuning them as we went along. We enjoy eating them as much as cooking them and many have become weekly favorites.

ENJOY!

RAMEKIN RECIPES

SPINACH PIE

This is an excellent version of the classic Spanakopita, but it's easy to make. If you serve it fresh from the oven it will sag a bit on the plate. I like to make it a few hours or even a day ahead and cool it in the fridge. When you do this the pie solidifies a little and after reheating it will stand up on it's own nicely. You can even make small versions of this pie in a mini muffin pan and serve them as appetizers (reduce and check the cooking time). A nice white pino grigo and a small salad and you've a great dinner. Kalí óreksi!

Ingredients

3 tbs. virgin olive oil

1 tsp. finely chopped garlic

½ cup diced onion

1 frozen chopped spinach (10 oz. pkg.)

1 egg beaten

4 oz. cottage cheese

½ tsp. oregano

Dash of salt and pepper

2 dashes each, cardamom and tumeric

1½ cup mozzarella cheese (shredded)

¼ cup seasoned bread crumbs

1 pkg. filo dough defrosted (need 4 sheets)

2 slices tomato (for top - optional)

Directions

Preheat oven to 350° F

Remove frozen spinach and one sleeve of the filo dough from freezer (most filo dough packages have two sleeves in a package) and allow them to defrost 2-4 hours. You can use the microwave to defrost the spinach, but not the filo, it turns brittle.

After the spinach and filo have defrosted, lightly sauté the garlic and onion in a small fry pan by first heating the oil, add the garlic, let it cook for a minute, add the onion, stir, cover and remove from the heat. By the time you're ready for it the onion will have cooked through.

Using a strainer in the sink, press all of the water out of the defrosted spinach (use your hand, press, flip, press again, repeat). Put two thirds of this in a large bowl. Add the beaten egg, cottage cheese, oregano, salt and pepper, cardamom, tumeric, mozzarella cheese, and the bread crumbs to the bowl and mix. Now add the garlic, onion, and oil mixture from the pan and mix thoroughly.

Spray PAM in both ramekins and spread it around with a paper towel lightly coating the entire inside. Open the sleeve of filo and pull out the roll, open the roll and remove two sheets of filo. Form a "V" shape with the filo and press it into the cup (be careful it rips easily) and let the extra droop over the sides.

Spoon the mixture into the cup until it is full and press down to remove any air. Now fold the excess filo up onto the top of the cup. Press the top lightly to further compact it. Now do the second one the same way. (You can also make this crust less, but you'll probably have to eat it out of the cup, (No filo? Try a little bread crumbs on top for browning). You can roll up the remaining filo dough, put it back in the sleeve and refreeze it for your next recipe. You can cover the ramekins and put them in the fridge for later baking if you wish.

Put them into your 350° F preheated oven and bake for 30 minutes or until the tops brown nicely. Cool for about five minutes, run a knife around the inside edges, flip them over onto a plate to remove, flip them back on your serving plate and add the slice of tomato to the top (if you wish). Serve with a nice green salad (olive oil and white balsamic vinegar dressing) and a glass of Chardonnay or Pinot Grigio. Enjoy!

CRAB CAKES

These are the best crab cakes ever for those who dream of giant chunks of crab. Use the giant lump crab - a 6 oz. can costs about $15 but it is very worth it. You can also use other crab but it just won't be the same. For another variation slice 4-5 jumbo shrimp into large chunks and use this instead of the jumbo crab. It really adds something to the crab cake. If you add the shrimp it will easily make four cakes. These freeze very well and we think they are even better after freezing.

Ingredients

1 can regular crab meat for flavor

1 can jumbo crab meat for texture

2 eggs beaten

¼ cup finely chopped onion

1 tsp. diced fresh basil (or ½ dried)

2 dashes each of paprika, cayenne pepper, garlic powder and salt

½ cup seasoned bread crumbs

¼ stick of butter melted

1 or 2 tbs. of lemon juice

4 sheets of filo dough

2 slices of tomato (optional) or a sprig of fresh basil

Directions

Preheat oven to 350° F

Place a frozen filo sleeve (there are usually two in a package) out to defrost. This will take a couple of hours. I usually just put this out to defrost in the morning and refrigerate it until needed. Do not microwave to defrost as it will make the sheets brittle. You can roll the unused sheets back up into the sleeve and refreeze when you are done.

When the filo has defrosted:

Open the cans of crab meat and drain them but keep them separate (the regular crab is for the flavor, the large lumps are for texture and big chunk bite). Jumbo shrimp can serve the same purpose or even enhance the cake. Cut the shrimp into large chunks and press them dry between paper towels

Beat two eggs in a medium bowl. Add the regular crab meat, bread crumbs, onion, basil, spices, salt, ½ of the melted butter, a teaspoon of lemon juice and mix well.

Oil two ramekins with PAM (or a drop of olive oil in each) then wipe out the excess with a paper towel.

Unroll the filo dough and remove two sheets. Form a "V" shape with the leaves and press the sheets gently into the bottom of the cup and let the overflow fall around the cup. Put a layer of the large lump meat in the bottom and add ½ of the remaining butter. Then fill the cup with the regular meat mixture. Press firmly to pack the crab mixture in and force out any air. Fold the filo from the sides over the top of the cake and press again. Do this again for the second cake.

Bake for about 30 min. or until the top turns brown. Top with a slice of tomato, dash of salsa or a sprig of fresh basil if desired.

Serve with a nice green salad (olive oil and white balsamic vinegar dressing) and a glass of Pinot Grigio. You can add a good seafood cocktail sauce or make your own with ¼ cup of ketchup and ½ teaspoon of ground horseradish. Some people even like them with hot Chinese style mustard or Wasabi. Enjoy!

NOODLES LORRAINE

This is a great meal for a cool night - Winter, Spring or Fall. There simply isn't anything that says "Comfort Food" better than egg noodles, ham and melted swiss cheese. The ramekins keeps it portionized so it's not a big dinner casserole. Serve it with a small salad or your favorite vegetable and a dry white wine. You can substitute cooked left over chicken or turkey meat if you don't like ham.

Ingredients

1 cup egg noodles (I like the curly ones)

1 egg beaten

1 medium onion diced

1 tbs. butter

Dash of salt

½ cup chopped ham or bacon (I use chopped up lunch meat or ham steak)

½ cup chopped swiss cheese

¼ cup parmesan cheese

Dash of nutmeg

Directions

Preheat oven to 375° F

Heat water to boiling in a medium sized saucepan. Add the noodles and cook until they just begin to soften (al dente) about 5 minutes. Rinse the noodles in cool water, drain and set aside.

Heat the butter in a small frying pan and sauté the onions until they turn transparent (don't brown them). In a large bowl mix the ham, cheeses and a dash of salt together and add the egg. Add the noodles, then the onion and mix it all thoroughly. Spray three or four Ramekins with PAM and wipe out any excess with a paper towel.

Pack each ramekin with the mixture a little above the rim. Sprinkle a small amount of nutmeg on top for color (if you are using ham, use paprika if chicken). Bake for about 20 - 30 min. Check often. The tops should be just turning brown on the edge of the exposed noodles when they are done.

These go very well with a full-bodied Chardonnay! Bon Appetit.

LASAGNA

This is a great Italian favorite. The secret to this is to keep the cheese layers very thin so you can build four or more noodle layers. Makes four small ramekins! Freeze the extras. They're even better the second time around. Serve it with a good Chianti and a small salad.

Ingredients

5 or 6 regular wide lasagna noodles
1 egg
½ cup ricotta cheese
1 cup mozzarella cheese
½ tsp. fresh garlic
   (can be left out if you don't like garlic)
½ tsp. oregano
Dash of nutmeg
Salt & pepper to taste
½ cup seasoned bread crumbs
1 cup of your favorite spaghetti sauce
PAM spray

Vegetarian Option
Add very finely chopped and lightly cooked, red/green pepper, onion, zucchini, carrot, egg plant, whatever you like to the cheese mix
.
Meat Option
Add cooked chopped hamburger, sausage, pepperoni, salami, etc. to the spaghetti sauce.

Directions

Preheat oven to 350° F

Cook the lasagna noodles in boiling water with a dash of olive oil and salt until they are limp. Using one of your ramekins, cut rounds out of the noodles by pressing and twisting an upside down ramekin on the noodle. You will need about three or four rounds for each ramekin.

To make the cheese layers, beat the egg in a bowl and add the ricotta cheese, ¾ of the mozzarella (reserve some for the top), garlic, oregano, nutmeg, bread crumbs, salt and pepper. (Plus your meat or vegetable options.)

Spray the ramekins lightly with PAM or coat lightly with olive oil. Now put one round in each ramekin. Add about 1 tbs. of the cheese layer, press it down and keep it thin. Then add another noodle round. Continue until you have just enough room for one more layer (the top). Put a splash of the spaghetti sauce and some mozzarella on top for color. For a meat version add cooked hamburger to the filling or pieces of pepperoni on top.

Heat the rest of the spaghetti sauce in a pan to provide it as a sauce for the lasagna when you serve it.

Bake for 30 min. or until the top browns up a little.

These are better if you let them rest for a few hours or at least ten minutes or so to thicken up. Just reheat if they grow cold before serving. Carefully (these will be hot!) cut around the edges of the ramekin with a knife to release the lasagna from the cup. Turn the cup upside down onto a small plate and then flip them onto their serving plate. Put the spaghetti sauce in a cute bowl with a spoon and allow your guests to add it as they wish. Enjoy!

CHICKEN POT PIE

Wonderful comfort food and you don't have to fool around with chicken stock, flour, butter and crème to get a good pie. If you don't have leftover chicken, sauté some chicken tenderloins or other chicken parts you like. Remember to remove the tendon from the tenderloin that runs thru it. Simply hold the tendon and scrape the meat off with a sharp knife held on an edge. Makes about 3 servings. Best served in the ramekin.

Ingredients

1 egg beaten

¾ cup left over cooked chicken, chopped
  or sauté some fresh

½ cup frozen mixed vegetables (carrots,
  peppers, green beans, peas, corn) defrosted and coarsely chopped if they are large

1 tbs. olive oil

¼ cup finely chopped onion

¼ cup finely chopped celery

1 can small potatoes - ¼ cup chopped

1 can of Campbell's Cream of Chicken soup

1/2 cup of water

Pepper to taste (the soup may have
  enough salt already)

Dash of garlic powder

Dash of thyme

1 roll of frozen filo dough defrosted

Directions

Preheat oven to 350° F

Saute the raw onion and celery in the olive oil until soft. Add the chicken, potato and vegetables just to warm them. Pour in the chicken soup, egg and water.

Mix and remove from heat. Add the spices. Fill the ramekins to the top with the mixture.

Bake for 25 minutes on a top rack of your oven. Put a cookie sheet on a lower rack (don't put the ramekins on this sheet) to catch any drippings. Roll 4 or 5 sheets of Filo dough into a tube and cut it up into ½ slices. After 25 minutes place a mound of the Filo dough on top of each ramekin and bake for about 5 min. more or until browned.

Serve this in the cup with a small salad, a good Merlot is a fine combination for a meal like this. Remind everyone that the cups are hot!

BEEF STEW

Beef stew really needs to cook for hours to make the beef chunks so tender they just fall apart in your mouth. I was going to eliminate it from this book until I discovered a work around. Buy frozen, pre-cooked, beef tips in the grocery store! They've already been slow cooked and work perfectly. Break about a cup or so of the frozen beef chunks out of the bag, don't bother with the gravy and leave the rest frozen for the next time. Then use Cream of Mushroom soup instead of beef broth with a little red wine added for color. A great beef stew in less than an hour!

Ingredients

1 tbs. of butter
1 tbs. olive oil

¼ cup onion
½ small clove of garlic crushed or a
   few dashes of garlic powder
1 can Cream of Mushroom soup
   but use only ½ can of water in it

¼ cup each coarsely chopped potato,
   celery, carrots, mushroom, green beans,
   and/or whatever else you might like, or you
   can just use a cup of frozen vegetable mix.
   Defrost these first for a few hours.
1 box/bag frozen pre-cooked beef tips -
   1 cup defrosted/chopped into 1" chunks
Black pepper
2 tbs. red wine
PAM spray
4-5 filo dough sheets defrosted. Roll the filo
   into a tube and slice it into ¼ inch rounds,
   then separate it into strips.

Directions

Preheat oven to 350° F

Heat the oil in a fry pan, add the butter and sauté the garlic, then onion. Add the vegetables, pepper and cook until they are just a little soft. Add the Cream of Mushroom soup with its water.

Heat the mixture slightly. Add the beef tips and about 2 tablespoons of red wine. Cook for a couple of minutes.

Spray two or three ramekins with PAM and spoon the mixture into them. Pack lots of beef and vegetables into each one and only a little gravy. Put a cookie sheet on the lower rack of your oven, these tend to boil over.

Place in the oven for about 30 min. Then pile the filo dough strips on top and bake about five more minutes or until top browns.

EGGPLANT PARMESAN

This one of our favorite vegetable meals. You could add a little hamburger to the sauce or some sausage or pepperoni on top for a garnish, if you wish. I like to put a little parmesan cheese on top before serving to dress it up.

Ingredients

1 medium eggplant

1 egg

2 tbs. of milk

½ cup Italian-style bread crumbs
   on a dinner plate

½ cup oil

½ clove of garlic crushed (optional)

8 oz. shredded mozzarella cheese

1 jar of your favorite spaghetti sauce

Oregano to taste

Directions

Preheat oven to 350° F

Peel the eggplant and cut it into ¼ inch thick rounds. Place a ramekin on top of the round and press out a circle which will fit in the ramekin. Make about six or eight of these. In a medium bowl, beat the egg and add the milk. Dip the eggplant rounds into the mixture and dredge them in the plate of bread crumbs, coat both sides and place them on a clean plate. Heat the oil in a large frying pan and when it is hot, sauté the garlic lightly (optional). Add the eggplant and cook until they are light brown on both sides. Place on a paper towel to drain.

Oil 3 or 4 ramekins with a coating of olive oil wipe out any excess with a paper towel. Put about a level tablespoon of spaghetti sauce in the bottom and cover it with an eggplant round. Put another tablespoon of sauce on top of this and enough Mozzarella to cover this - about a tablespoon full. Then sprinkle some oregano on top. Repeat the eggplant, sauce, mozzarella, oregano until the ramekin is full. The top layer should end with cheese and oregano.

Put the ramekins on a cookie sheet as they may overflow, bake for about 30 minutes. Serve these in the cup as they just turn to a pile of mush if you try to remove them. Enjoy them with a nice salad and a robust Italian red wine like Chianti or Valpollicella.

ENCHILADA IN A CUP

Great for Cinco de Mayo or any occasion that calls for Mexican! Serve with a salad or your favorite vegetables... These make great appetizers on game day too!

Ingredients

1 small bag of round corn tortilla chips
  (any shape will do)
1 small can of enchilada sauce
  (mild, medium, hot, whatever you like)
¼ lb. hamburger
½ tsp. minced garlic
¼ cup minced onion
½ cup sharp cheddar cheese
1 pkg. taco seasoning mix
Salt, pepper, garlic powder, PAM spray

Directions

Preheat oven to 350° F

Break up about a dozen or so of the corn chips into small pieces.

Saute the hamburger in a small fry pan with a little oil, add the minced garlic and a little salt and pepper. Break it up to a fine consistency. When it is just about done add two tablespoons of the taco seasoning mix and finish cooking. Cover with a lid.

Make a mixture of the hamburger, ¼ cup of the enchilada sauce, the minced onion, the sharp cheddar cheese, a couple of dashes of the garlic powder and a dash or so of salt and pepper.

Spray 2 or 3 ramekins with PAM and put a thin layer of the chips into the bottom of each cup. Add about a heaping tablespoon of the mix to the cups and press it down flat. Now add another thin layer of chips and another layer of the mix. Repeat until the cups are almost full. For the top (the last layer) put a heaping tablespoon of the enchilada sauce covered with sharp cheddar and a sprinkle of the taco seasoning mix for color.

Bake in the oven at 350 degrees for about 30 minutes or until the top has browned slightly (begin checking after 20 minutes). Place a couple of broken taco chips on top.

Serve in the ramekins with taco chips for dunking (if you wish), but warn everyone they are hot!

MINI MEATLOAF

Meatloaf is a great treat on a cold winters night. The only problem with it is there is just so much of it left over. Here's an easy portion control meatloaf that will serve for dinner and even a couple of sandwiches the next day. Keep in mind that you won't need any filo dough liner or even PAM spray. The hamburger makes enough oil all by itself to make the mini loaf release. I cut up a sheet of Filo into ½ inch strips , arrange them into a rough cap on top about five minutes before the loafs are done and they will make a fine crunchy brown top for the loafs.

Ingredients

1 egg beaten

¾ lb. or so of hamburger

   (makes about four mini meat loafs)

¼ cup finely chopped onion

¼ cup finely chopped green pepper (optional)

½ clove of garlic, crushed (optional) or

   two dashes of garlic salt

2 tbs. of ketchup

¼ cup seasoned bread crumbs

1 tbs. of Worcestershire sauce

Dash of sage

Dash of dry mustard

Salt and pepper to taste

   (leave out salt if garlic salt used)

Directions

Preheat Oven to 350° F

Beat the egg for a minute or so. Then add the hamburger (if you only want to make two loafs use ½ lb of hamburger). Add the rest of the ingredients stirring to mix as you do so. Then mix it all together thoroughly with your hands, squeezing it to make a smooth mixture. Put enough of the mixture into each ramekin to fill it almost to the top.

Bake for about 25 minutes, then add the topping and bake until light brown for about five more minutes. You should be able to pick the loaf out of the cup using two forks. Serve with a nice green salad or your favorite vegetable.

PIZZA IN A CUP

There is nothing like a really good pizza. The only problem is that even a small one is too big for one or two people. You can always go out for a slice but those tend to be dry and soft... not what you were really looking for. Look no more, pizza in a cup is small enough for one, has no fattening crust and has exactly the toppings you want, because you pick them out! Pull some green and red peppers, mozzarella, pepperoni, mushrooms what ever you want from the fridge and you're ready to go. Crack open a bottle of chianti and you have your own Italian restaurant at home.

Ingredients

1 tbs. olive oil

1 cup or so of your favorite Italian sauce

1 cup mozzarella cheese shredded

¼ cup Parmesan cheese shredded or dry

Small amounts (¼ cup) each coarsely
   chopped: onions, cooked peppers, cooked
   mushrooms, black olives, sautéed
   hamburger, cooked sausage, pepperoni,
   salami, ham, anchovies, pineapple, you
   name it. These are very custom pizzas

Oregano, salt and pepper

Red pepper if you wish

Directions

Preheat Oven to 350° F

Wipe the inside of a couple of ramekins with some of the olive oil. This will make them easier to clean when you're done. Put the rest in a bowl. Add the tomato sauce, parmesan cheese, ¼ of the mozzarella and your selection of toppings, retain pepperoni , salami or pineapple for the top if you're going to use them. Salt and pepper to taste. Mix this all together and fill a ramekin leaving room for the topping mozzarella.

Put a mound of mozzarella on top and decorate the top with a couple of slices of pepperoni, peppers, broccoli or what ever you like. Sprinkle the top with some oregano and you're ready to go.

Bake for 30 minutes or until the cheese begins to brown on top.

Enjoy with a good Valpolichello or a chianti and dream of a vacation to Italy!

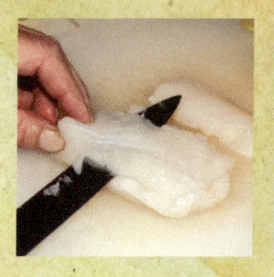

GERMAN FISH PIE

If you love the classic white fish chowder or just fish and mashed potatoes, this dish is for you. Unlike many of the recipes, this one is actually served in the cup so you will only need a few sheets of filo dough sliced into ribbons to form an attractive topping for the dish. You cook the dish through and then add the shredded filo dough to the top. Cook it about five minutes more until the filo browns and serve.

Ingredients

1 tbs. olive oil and 1 pat of butter

½ cup finely chopped onion

1 tsp. flour

1 pint cream (milk just doesn't work)

A couple of dashes of salt
  and a dash or two of pepper

Dash or two of dry dill

1 or two small flounder, cod or other white
  fish fillets about ½ lb. (Check carefully for
  bones) If you buy a thick filet slice it into
  ¼ inch thick strips. Cut the strips to fit into
  the cup.

1 large potato, peeled and sliced very thin
  (a little thicker than a potato chip).

2 or 3 sheets of filo dough

Directions

Preheat Oven to 350° F

Heat the olive oil and butter in a small fry pan and sauté the onion until just transparent. Add the flour, dill, salt and pepper and mix it thoroughly to create a smooth mixture. This will create a thickener which will not lump up in your dish. Add the cream and constantly stirring, just heat it enough to begin thickening it. Remove the pan from the heat.

Put a tablespoon of the mixture into the bottom of the ramekin. Then put a slice of potato in to cover the bottom, then another tablespoon of mix, then a slice of fish. Alternate until you have almost reached the top and make the final layer of mix.

Put a cookie sheet or a sheet of tin foil on the shelf under the ramekins as they may bubble over and put them on the upper shelf of your oven.

Cook for 20 minutes, then put the cut up strips of Filo on top and bake for another 10 minutes until golden brown.

Serve with oyster crackers and a nice green salad and you're all set. A full bodied white Bordeaux goes nicely with this dish, but Chardonnay or Pinot Grigio is great too.

SALMON POT PIE

If you love the taste of salmon and pot pies, this may be the dish for you. A creamy fish base with the refreshing tang of chicken broth and potato that brings out the clean, sea salt taste of fresh salmon.

Ingredients

1 lb. of fresh Salmon, skin removed cut
   into 1" chunks

¼ cup coarsely chopped canned potato

¼ cup each fresh onion, carrot, celery and
   mushroom or frozen mixed vegetables
   (about ¾ cup total)

¼ cup olive oil

1 oz. melted Butter

2 Tbs. Flour

1 cup of chicken stock

1 TBS white wine

½ cup cream

A small amount of crushed garlic
   and a sprinkling of dill

Salt and pepper to taste

PAM spray

4 - 5 filo dough sheets defrosted. Roll the
   filo into a tube and slice it into ¼ inch
   rounds and separate it into strips

Directions

Preheat Oven to 350° F

In a sauté pan, cook the vegetables in the oil until they are soft or if you are using frozen until they just defrost.

Mix the butter and the flour in the sauté pan and cook to mix them together. Add the cream and the chicken stock.

Add the salmon and cook until it just becomes opaque. Add the chopped potato and vegetables, garlic powder, salt and pepper. Cook it on low heat stirring constantly until it begins to thicken.

PAM spray two or three ramekins and fill them with the mixture, leaving a little space on top. Try to get lots of Salmon in each cup, not lots of liquid.

Put a cookie sheet on the lower rack of your oven as these tend to boil over. Place in the oven for about 30 minutes then pile the filo dough strips on top and bake about five more minutes or until top browns.

VEGETABLE POT PIE

This is a nice vegetable dish, a great change of pace when you get tired of meat and you want something different. Not a truly vegetarian dish as it does contain butter, cheese and soup, without these it is just a little too bland for our taste. Pretty easy to make, we tend to just use any vegetables we have on hand or left over from other dishes. You can also use frozen vegetables, but saute them very quickly (if at all) as you want the veggies to be a little al dente. Give it a try, you'll really like it.

Ingredients

1 tbs. of butter
1 tbs. olive oil
¼ cup onion
½ small clove of garlic crushed or a
    few dashes of garlic powder
1 can Cream of Mushroom soup but use
    only ½ can of water in it.
¼ cup each coarsely chopped potato, celery,
    carrots, mushroom, green beans, and/or
    whatever else you might like, or you can
    just use a cup of frozen vegetable mix.
    Defrost these first for a few hours. Cut the
    large pieces into smaller bits. We like to
    use a stew blend that has a little potato in
    it and the Southwest blend that has corn
    and peppers in it.
1/8 tsp. Oregano
Salt and pepper to taste
¼ cup shredded parmesan
½ cup mozzarella, or sharp cheddar cheese
    depending on your taste

Directions

Preheat Oven to 350° F

Heat the oil in a fry pan, add the butter and sauté the garlic, then onion. Add the vegetables, oregano, salt and pepper and cook until they are just a little soft.

Add the Cream of Mushroom soup with its water. Heat the mixture slightly.

Fill a ramekin and place some of the cheese on top. Bake for 30 minutes or until the top browns Serve in the cup. Makes 2-3 ramekins. For decoration, you can make strips out of filo or a flour tortilla and place them like an apple pie on top.

Enjoy with a nice Pinot Grigo. Bon Appetite!

CUP O' CALZONE

Calzone is one of those dishes that you can make with any filling you wish. We did this recipe with just about everything, salami, ham, peppers, onion, spinach and a ton of mozzarella cheese, even a touch of spaghetti sauce. You can make yours with the fillings you wish, classic meat or spinach and mushroom. The trick is to stuff the grande burrito with a lot of filling. Roll up the burrito wrapper and cut rounds out of it kind of like a "Futomaki" or a giant sushi roll. You want to wind up with about a 2.5 inch width roll or so to fill the average ramekin.

Ingredients

1 grande flour burrito taco
6 slices large salami lunch meat
6 slices ham lunch meat
1/3 cup spaghetti sauce (optional)
1/3 cup diced onion
1/3 cup julienned red pepper microwaved
   or sauteed for a minute until soft
1/2 cup chopped mushrooms microwaved
   or sautéed for a minute or so
1 cup spinach microwaved or sautéed for
   a minute or so down to ¼ cup
3/4 cup Mozzarella
Couple of dashes of oregano
Couple of dashes of garlic powder and
   pepper to taste
Splash of olive oil for the top
PAM spray

Directions

Preheat Oven to 350° F

Place a grande flour taco on a cutting board. Spread the Spaghetti sauce to cover the burrito (optional). Spread the salami around keeping it to the bottom 2/3 of the burrito. Add the vegetables and the spinach. Put the ham on top of this on the bottom 2/3 of the burrito. Put the Mozzarella on top of this and sprinkle with the garlic powder, pepper and oregano to the bottom 2/3 of the burrito

Now roll the burrito up into a tight, large roll. Leave the seam on the bottom. Cut 2.5" or so rounds out of the roll and place them face down in a PAM sprayed ramekin. Take any left over trimmings from your cutting board or add some more cheese to the top. Put a dash of olive oil on top. The center will shrink down a little as it cooks and you should wind up with a nice brown rim. Cook for about 30 minutes at 350 degrees checking for brown-ness after 20.

These are excellent hot or cold. Hot from the oven they seem more like pizza, probably due to the spaghetti sauce. Cold they are very calzone like. We think they make an excellent cold lunch side dish cut into quarters with a salad. If it's a bright sunny day, try a nice chardonnay. Enjoy!

FRITTATA

A Frittata is much like a solid scrambled egg, but it is usually cooked slowly in a fry pan until the bottom just solidifies, then the cheese etc. is added on top and the pan is put under the broiler until the top cooks. The dish swells up with the steam and makes a beautiful presentation at a special breakfast. We developed this ramekin version to make it an easy to bake dish, makes 2-3 servings.

Ingredients

3 eggs

½ cup of milk

1 tbs. flour

¼ cup chopped onion

¾ cup shredded mozzarella cheese
    loosely packed

Pepper to taste (mozzarella has salt in it)

A couple of pinches of oregano

Mozzarella cheese for the top

1 small cooked asparagus tip or a small
    cherry tomato slice for a garnish

PAM or Olive Oil

Directions

Preheat Oven to 350° F

Beat the eggs in a small bowl. We use a hand blender or mixer on high for this. Beat in the milk and flour with the blender or mixer. Fold in gently by hand, the onion, mozzarella cheese, pepper and oregano.

Pour the mixture into a greased ramekin. Put some mozzarella on top, sprinkle with a dash of oregano and add the garnish

Bake at 350 degrees for 30 minutes. Put the garnish on top and serve.

Run a thin knife around the edges to release the Frittata. Pour it onto a plate and flip it back over to serve. Serve it with a small salad and champagne, enjoy!

QUICHE LORRAINE

A Sunday morning delight. This is light and easy and is a special change from the usual cereal or bacon and eggs.

Ingredients

¼ cup chopped green pepper – cooked

¼ cup chopped broccoli – cooked

¼ cup chopped mushrooms – cooked

¼ cup chopped onions - cooked

½ cup ham lunch meat chopped

2 eggs beaten

½ cup shredded cheddar cheese

¼ cup milk

¼ cup pancake mix, Bisquick or flour

Salt and pepper to taste

Dash of nutmeg

Directions

Preheat Oven to 375° F

We put all of the vegetables into a dish and cook them in the microwave for a few minutes. Let them cool before continuing. You can also sauté the vegetables in a fry pan and a little olive oil. Cook them until they have softened.

In a medium bowl, beat the two eggs. Add the lunch meat, cheddar cheese, milk and pancake mix. Add the cooled vegetables (if you add them when they are hot they will cook the eggs) and the nutmeg, salt and pepper. Mix thoroughly.

Spray two ramekins with PAM and fill them with the mixture. You may have enough left over for three or four ramekins.

Bake for 25 minutes until lightly browned on top. Start checking them after 20 minutes.

Run around the edges with a butter knife and they should pop out of the ramekin. If they should stick spoon them out of the cup and put the top on top. They'll still taste delicious!

There are a many variations you can try, crab meat, lobster, smoked salmon, sausage, bacon, swiss cheese instead of cheddar, use mozzarella or Provolone cheese on top. Be creative.

This is another dish that makes excellent mini versions for a breakfast buffet or as an appetizer. Make a double batch or two of three versions and cook them in mini muffin pans. Be careful, these will cook very quickly and you don't want to burn them.

Goes great with Bloody Marys or a nice Pinot Grigio, perhaps Champagne?

Enjoy.

POACHED EGGS

If you know how to poach an egg, you can skip this. But if you have problems poaching an egg or if you're like Julie in "Julie and Julia" and your eggs fail then read on. First of all you don't just crack an egg from two feet in the air into a pot of boiling water. You put the shelled egg into a greased soup ladle, place the ladle into the boiling water for about 15 seconds and then gently pour it into the pot. Or you can use our method!

Ingredients

Ramekins or rubber poaching cups
PAM spray for the ramekins or cups
1 egg per ramekin or cup
Pinch of salt for the water

You'll also need:
Pot with 1 inch boiling water and lid.
We use a sauté pan for this.
Tongs

Directions

Spray the ramekin with PAM and crack an egg into it.

Place the ramekin into a pot with about an inch of gently boiling water with a dash of salt (use tongs or gloves and a low sided pan).

Put a lid on it and cook for 4 minutes for very soft boiled, 5 minutes for soft and 6 minutes for hard boiled. Add one minute if you are using the rubber poaching cups.

Pour the egg out on a paper towel to drain the water off, then flip it onto a plate for serving.

Put it on top of a piece of buttered toast or a half English muffin, yum! It will be the buttery-est, best-tasting egg you've ever eaten. A great summer dinner with a large green salad. We like the rubber poaching cups you can get at Crate and Barrel. They are perfect for this as they have handles and they make an attractive mountain shape out of the egg.

21637484R00026

Printed in Poland
by Amazon Fulfillment
Poland Sp. z o.o., Wrocław